60 YEARS OF THE
Chinese Zodiac

LEON P. BURNETTE

Copyright © 2018 by Leon P. Burnette.

All rights reserved. No part of this publication may be reproduced, distributed, or transmitted in any form or by any means, including photocopying, recording, or other electronic or mechanical methods, without the prior written permission of the author, except in the case of brief quotations embodied in critical reviews and certain other noncommercial uses permitted by copyright law.

Printed in the United States of America

ISBN: Paperback: 978-1-948172-34-9
eBook: 978-1-948172-33-2

Library of Congress Control Number: 2018937634

Stonewall Press
363 Paladium Court
Owings Mills, MD 21117
www.stonewallpress.com
1-888-334-0980

*Dedicated to my friends of the Northern
Dance Force and Anoka Hockey Band*

CONTENTS

RAT 9
OX 13
TIGER 17
RABBIT (CAT) 21
DRAGON 27
SNAKE 33
HORSE 39
SHEEP 45
MONKEY 51
ROOSTER 55
DOG 59
BOAR 63

Chinese horoscopes are influenced by the five elements, fire water, metal, wood, and earth.

EARTH
Earth elements give stability and practicality.

WATER
Water elements gives sensitivity and persuasiveness.

WOOD
Wood elements give greater creativity and imagination powers.

METAL
Metal elements gives added willpower and stronger character.

FIRE
Fire elements gives added passion and impulsive energy.

Green — Help Growth
Red — conflicts

Fire

Wood

Earth

Water

Metal

RAT

Resourceful and clever, the Rat is seen as a positive animal. Both as intelligent and daring; finding a way to success. You do have a stronger drive for power and money.

RAT FACT

First animal in the order

Chinese Name	:	SHU sign of charm
Western Counterpart	:	Sagittarius
Color	:	Light Blue
Gemstones	:	Diamonds, Amethyst
Good Friend	:	Dragons, Monkeys
Bad Friends	:	Horses

CHARACTERISTICS

Good	:	Charisma, Quick-wittedness, Sociability, Intelligence
Bad	:	Greed, Secretiveness, Acquisitiveness

LOVE CONNECTION

Rat : Physically great, conflicting emotions and issues
Ox : Mutually happy, better as an affair
Tiger : Little passion, Tempers clash
Sheep : Hard battle, both need to be willing to fight
Dragon: Heavenly relationship, full of passion
Snake : Once learning each other's way, good with work
Horse : Very unstable, like oil and water
Monkey: Great sharing and understanding
Rooster: Too many problems no love lost here
Dog : Boring but solid, full of respect
Pig : Good friends but a relationship of ups and downs

METAL RAT

Years of Metal Rat: 1900, 1960, 2020

You have a strong purpose and ideals. But it can lead you to strong emotions both good and bad. Being in charge is where you want to be. And take great happiness in having good taste in decorating your home and work place.

Famous Metal Rats: Morten Anderson, Antonio Banderas, Chuck D.

WATER RAT

Years of Water Rat: 1912, 1972, 2032

These rats have a gift for influencing people. Great thinker and problem solvers. Liked and respected by others.

Famous Water Rats: Manny Ramirez, Brad Paisley, Eric Dane, Jennifer Garner, Alyssa Milano, Carmen Electra

WOOD RAT

Years of Wood Rat: 1924, 1984, 2044

Hides their true faces, not known of having confidence from all the other wood rats. Often worrying about failures. With family around they are friendly and protective.

Famous Wood Rats: Yanin Vismitananda, Tom Landry, Lauren Bacall, Ashlee Simpson

FIRE RAT

Years of Fire Rat: 1936, 1996, 2056

You have a touch of impulsiveness. And a love of travel keeps you always on the move. Never happy with routines, and are always looking for the next adventure.

Famous Fire Rats: James Lee Burke, Ursula Andress, Joe Don Baker

EARTH RAT

Years of Earth Rat: 1948, 2008, 2068

The Earth Rat is very reversed and a good achiever. You will get your roots set early in a good future with you and family. With a feet on the earth mind to ideals and business. Can be stingy but will have good steady gain in money.

Famous Earth Rats: Aaron Brown, Barbara Mandrell, Patti Austin, Andrew Lloyd Webber

OX

People born under the year of the Ox, are very practical and down to earth. Steady and very persistent. Impatient, sulky and narrow-minded.

OX FACTS

Second animal in the order

Chinese Name   : NIU sign of industry
Month   : January
Western Counterpart : Capricorn
Color   : Violet
Gemstones   : Jade, Emerald
Good Friends   : Roosters, Snakes
Bad Friends   : Sheep

CHARACTERISTICS

Good : Honesty, Loyalty, Reliability, Steadfastness
Bad : Stubbornness, Sulkiness, Inflexibility

LOVE CONNECTION

Rat	:	Great at love affairs, but no long term relationships
Ox	:	Solid relationship; best ground for growing a great marriage
Tiger	:	Opposites attract, but despite the great start these may be the worse relationship present
Rabbit	:	Easy and happy family life
Dragon	:	Locking horns on most things
Snake	:	In synch together, very understanding and loving
Horse	:	Bad bed partners maybe better as business partners
Sheep	:	Not even in your dreams
Monkey	:	If you can make this relationship work, life will be truly fun and happy
Rooster	:	Good match full of love and passion
Dog	:	Not good, but there's always hope
Pig	:	Worth the problems that may rise

METAL OX

Years of the Metal Ox: 1901, 1961, 2021

Very hard worker, but not known for showing lots of emotions. Will stop at nothing to achieve their goals and has the will power to see people through.

Famous Metal Oxen: Sebastian Coe, Toby Keith, Scott Baio, Woody Harrelson

WATER OX

Years of the Water Ox: 1913, 1973, 2033

You are hardworking and a quick thinker than other oxen with a more open-mind and sensitive making them easier to live with and great with friends and family.

Famous Water Oxen: Sasha Alexander, Kate Beckinsale, Aishwarya Rai, Alexa Doig, Yunjin Kim

WOOD OX

Years of the Wood Ox: 1925, 1985, 2045

Forgiving and fair-minded. You are more willing to accept change than most oxen. Great self-confidence and are known to make good leaders.

Famous Wood Oxen: Aya Ueto, Leona Lewis, Leon A. Burnette, FeFe Dobson, Kaley Cuaco

FIRE OX

Years of the Fire Ox: 1937, 1997, 2057

The fire in you gives you a strong urge to lead and dominate the situation. Hot tempered and can be impulsive in some actions.

Famous Fire Oxen: Madeleine K. Albright, Waylon Jennings, Merle Haggard, Bill Cosby

EARTH OX

Years of the Earth Ox: 1949, 2009, 2069

You are shrewd and have a good sense of judgment making for a success in business ventures. Others look up to you because you're willing to shoulder more than your share of the work.

Famous Earth Oxen: Christopher Hitchens, Bobby Clarke, Tom Watson, Armand Assante, Joyce Dewitt

TIGER

Tigers are full of energy and optimism. Even their most rash actions usually turn out well for them. Straight-forward yet sensitive. They are courageous and always alert to any dangers. And will fight bravely when needed to.

TIGER FACTS

Third animal in the order

Chinese Name	:	HU sign of courage
Western Counterpart	:	Aquarius
Color	:	Mid-green
Gemstones	:	Ruby, Cat's Eye
Best Friends	:	Horses, Dog
Bad Friends	:	Monkeys

CHARACTERISTICS

Good : Courage, boldness, energy, optimism
Bad : Vanity, Hot-headed, impulsiveness

LOVE CONNECTION

Rat	:	Good friends but passion is brief
Ox	:	Positive and negative attract, but beware when it goes boom
Tiger	:	Too many chiefs for this relationship to work
Rabbit	:	Here what makes you different is what makes this works
Dragon	:	All fireworks and passion
Snake	:	No meeting here in the middle or end
Horse	:	One exciting life and relationship
Sheep	:	Respectful at work, does not work in marriage
Monkey	:	You only drive your partner crazy
Rooster	:	Misunderstanding will happen if you do not talk your problems out. DOG : You are great team and have much success
Pig	:	Humor will keep this relationship going

METAL TIGER

Years of the Metal Tiger: 1950, 2010, 2070

Quicksilver thoughts and actions. Competitive and determined, you always stand out in a crowd. Need to keep your temper in control.

Famous Metal Tigers: Samuel A. Alito Jr., Debbie Allen, Tom Berenger, Gabriel Byrne, Peter Frampton

WATER TIGER

Years of the Water Tiger: 1902, 1962, 2022

Calmer than most tigers, you are endowed with insight and strong intuition. This tiger finds himself lost in thought instead of acting.

Famous Water Tigers: Michelle Yeoh, Bobby Jones, Paula Abdul, Joan Cusack

WOOD TIGER

Years of the Wood Tiger: 1914, 1974, 2034

You work with others better than most tigers. Warm and acceptable; popular with many friends. Will take charge if given a chance.

Famous Wood Tigers: Penelope Cruz, Hideki Matsui, Magglio Ordonez, Victoria Beckham, Alyson Hannigan, Grace Park

FIRE TIGER

Years of the Fire Tiger: 1926, 1986, 2046

You find yourself full of energy and passion. Your inborn powers of leadership help you thru your latest scheme.

Famous Fire Tigers: Cassie Ventura, Christian Burnette, Emma Rossum, Kat Denning, Linsdey Lohan, Amanda Bynes

EARTH TIGER

Years of the Earth Tiger: 1938, 1998, 2058

You don't get swept away easy about excitement. This tiger has a strong sense of responsibility. Be careful not to lose your sense of humor or stop caring about the feelings of others.

Famous Earth Tigers: Stephen Breyer, Sam Nunn, Oscar Robertson, Drew Carey

RABBIT (CAT)

Sometimes listed as the cat. The rabbits are quiet individuals often shy. But in contrast they are also a social creature by nature. Ready to chat or be in the company of others.

RABBIT FACTS

Fourth animal in the order

Western Counterpart	:	Pisces
Month	:	March
Color	:	Pale Green
Gemstones	:	Pearl, Crystal
Best Friends	:	Sheep, Pigs
Bad Friends	:	Roosters

CHARACTERISTICS

Good : Wisdom, Docility, Thoughtfulness, Refinement
Bad : Cunning, Snobbery, Possessiveness

LOVE CONNECTION

Rat	:	Better to keep your distant
Ox	:	You will have a calm and peaceful life
Tiger	:	Your differences will make a strong bond
Rabbit	:	Two parts of a whole, success is your
Dragon	:	For success you need a lot of give and take
Horse	:	Hard times but worth the effort
Sheep	:	Blissful, true love, shared understanding
Monkey	:	New meaning to heartbreak hotel
Rooster	:	No common ground
Dog	:	Solid as a rock
Pig	:	Could be the everlasting love

METAL RABBIT

Years of the Metal Rabbit: 1951, 2011, 2071

While timid you have a strong intuition and ambitious. With your cunning and shrewd behavior in business you go far. You give the same dedication in love as business. You lose your heart fast and deep in love.

Famous Metal Rabbits: Timothy Bottoms, Julie Kavner, Melissa Manchester

WATER RABBIT

Years of the Water Rabbit: 1903, 1963, 2023

More than willing to go along with the crowd. You like to avoid fights when able. Over sensitive. Watch that others do not take advantage of you

Famous Water Rabbits: Anita Mui, Joel Osteen, Lou Gehrig, Lisa Kudrow, Rob Schneider, Quentin Tarantino

WOOD RABBIT

Years of the Wood Rabbit: 1915, 1975, 2035

Popular and kind, you have a need and desire for peace more than others. You are not known for pitting a side, but like to sit and wait for the outcome. Very accommodating, you find it hard to hurt others feelings.

Famous Wood Rabbits: Trish Stasus, Asia Argento, Milla Jovovich, Fergie, Torrie Wilson

FIRE RABBIT

Years of the Fire Rabbit: 1927, 1987, 2047

Outgoing and bold you are the adventurer of the rabbit family. Born with strong diplomacy skills will help lead you into success. Watch your emotional outbursts, you have a surprising fiery when confronted.

Famous Fire Rabbits: Aya Hirano, Karen Gillan

EARTH RABBIT

Years of the Earth Rabbit: 1939, 1999, 2059

Logical and level minded. Careful in all their dealings. Giving others to believe in them. You value home comforts most. And works to achieve your desire for security and stability.

Famous Earth Rabbits: John Negroponte, Jane Alexander, Elizabeth Ashley, Phil Everly, William Friedkin

DRAGON

Colorful and exotic, it's the symbol of power and good fortune. Dragons do things in grand style. Confident and has full of energy. They face even challenges and often meet with great success. A charismatic presence, but sometimes too prideful to accept help when needed.

DRAGON FACTS

Fifth animal in the order

Chinese Name   : LONG sign of luck
Western Counterpart : Aries
Month   : April
Color   : Greenish-blue
Gemstones   : Opal, Sapphire, Amber
Friends   : Rats, Monkeys
Foes   : Dogs

CHARACTERISTICS

Good : Originality, Resourcefulness, Valor, Adaptability
Bad   : Arrogance, Hot-headed, Quick-tempered

LOVE CONNECTION

Rat	:	Passion and understanding will lead you to victory
Ox	:	This will only know success with all of give and take in the relationship
Tiger	:	Brave duo, lots of sparks and passion
Rabbit	:	How hard you fight will make or break this one
Dragon	:	Sharing is the key to this partnership
Snake	:	Clever and quick-witted you complete each other
Horse	:	Great sex will need more understanding to make it work
Sheep	:	Physically fun but nothing else going on
Monkey	:	Happiness and success is in the cards here
Rooster	:	Never dull, but beware, egos do not stop you
Dog	:	Walk away and do not look back
Pig	:	Deeply in love and caring

METAL DRAGON

Years of the Metal Dragon: 1940, 2000, 2060

Honest but insensitive. Respects those that stand up to them. Always looking for action while others are drawn to their charisma.

Famous Metal Dragons: James Clyburn, King Constantine II, Shirley Muldowney, Russell Banks, Bernardo Bertolucci, Barry Corbin, Martin Sheen, Percy Sledge

WATER DRAGON

Years of the Water Dragon: 1952, 2012, 2072

More thoughtful and sensitive than other dragons. You know more patience and able to watch things from the side line. Your failure comes when you don't research things or don't see them thru before starting anew.

Famous Water Dragons: John Tesh, Will Shortz, Susan Seidelman, George Strait, Stephen Lang

WOOD DRAGON

Years of the Wood Dragon: 1904, 1964, 2024

Practicality and a great deal of imagination comes with this sign. And you are still willing to listen to others ideals. While outspoken and even pushy to some, you do get along with others and are very successful when it involves your own comfort and contentment.

Famous Wood Dragons: Monica Bellucci, Laura Linney, John Leguizanamo, Melissa Gilbert, Robin Givens, Bridget Fonda

FIRE DRAGON

Years of the Fire Dragon: 1916, 1976, 2036

You are like two dragons in one. Able to go from calm to burning mad in 45 seconds. Sometimes you are your own worst enemy. Jumping to conclusions comes easy for you. Keep your passions and competitive temper under control.

Famous Fire Dragons: Qi Shu, Sarkira, Amy Acker, Piper Perabo, Emmanuelle Vangier, Zhao Wei, Stephenie Mcmanhanon

EARTH DRAGON

Years of the Earth Dragon: 1928, 1988, 2048

You have a flair for organizing, a strong urge to lead. Sociable and easier to approach than other dragons. Well worth the respect and loves your command.

Famous Earth Dragons: Donavan Burnette, Juan Martin del Potro, Ford Whitey, Rupert Grint, Vanessa Hudgens, Kevin McHale, Alexa Vega

SNAKE

Old folklore says "If you have a snake in your house you never stave." Snake people have a more than natural shrewdness in as to be called psychic. Cool tempered and enigmatic to others.

SNAKE FACTS

Sixth animal in the order

Chinese Name	:	SHE is the sign of sagacity
Month	:	May
Western Counterpart	:	Taurus
Color	:	Red
Gemstones	:	Topaz, Jasper, Bloodstone
Friends	:	Oxen, Roosters
Foes	:	Pigs

CHARACTERISTICS

Good : Insight, Shrewdness, Wisdom, Compassion
Bad : Malice, Vanity, Manipulation, Pride

LOVE CONNECTION

Rat	:	Very alluring but lots of work
Ox	:	Understanding and loving relationship
Tiger	:	Million to one shot
Rabbit	:	Deep passions and earth moving sex
Dragon	:	The piece that was missing now whole
Snake	:	Strong jealousy issues
Horse	:	Poor future even with help
Sheep	:	Great friends, better lovers
Monkey	:	Must learn trust for each other
Rooster	:	Go team go!!!
Dog	:	Good both physical and mental
Pig	:	Little to no common grounds

METAL SNAKE

Years of the Metal Snake: 1941, 2001, 2061

Extra-strong will-power. Lover of the finer things in life. Will always find a way to get into any group you want. Likes to act alone. And money is always important.

Famous Metal Snakes: L. Paul Bremer III, Pete Rose, Marv Albert, Joan Baez, Neil Diamond, Placido Domingo, Aaron Neville, Ryan O'neal

WATER SNAKE

Years of the Water Snake: 1953, 2013, 2073

Your insights are well in the psychic range. Extremely practical and intellectual, and have a great business mind. And have a natural secrecy to your nature. Loyal is the most strongest when family is involved.

Famous Water Snakes: Bill Pullman, Alfre Woodard, Tim Allan, Kim Basinger, Pat Benatar, Pierce Brosnan

WOOD SNAKE

Years of the Wood Snake: 1905, 1965, 2025

Not as narcissistic as the rest of snakes. The kindest of snake, with a love of family and friends. Seeks advice of others, never cope alone. Deep intellect and good at understanding of others. And great leaders.

Famous Wood Snakes: Leon P. Burnette, Elizabeth Hurley, Gong Li, Sherilyn Fenn, Peter Krause, Luke Perry

FIRE SNAKE

Years of the Fire Snake: 1917, 1977, 2037

Magnetic and charismatic are the best ways to describe this member of the snake family. With his power of persuasion, people hang on his every word. Like most snakes he has a love for money, and can be self-centered with a hard time trusting others.

Famous Fire Snakes: Gail Kim, Sarah M. Gellar, Gigi Edgely, Aki Hoshino, Zachary Quinto, Jamie Pressly

EARTH SNAKE

Years of the Earth Snake: 1929, 1989, 2049

Not as untrusting as the other snakes. Relaxed, outgoing and more honest than other snakes. And less likely to take big risks as others will. But still good as others for making money.

Famous Earth Snakes: Tabitha Burnette, Yumi Sugimoto, Max Von Sydow, Alia Shawkat, Daniel Radcliffe, Hayden Panettiere

HORSE

You are the life of the party. With great wit, Horses are attracted to the fine life. While independent you are loyal to friends without a thought.

HORSE FACTS

Seventh animal in the order

Chinese Name	:	MA is the sign of elegance
Month	:	June
Western Counterpart	:	Gemini
Color	:	Flame Orange
Gemstones	:	Amethyst, Turquoise, Topaz
Friends	:	Tiger, Dogs
Foes	:	Rats

CHARACTERISTICS

Good : Stamina, Wit, Independence, Cheerfulness
Bad : Vanity, Recklessness, Impatience, Selfishness

LOVE CONNECTION

Rat	:	Unstable relationship
Ox	:	Keep this business only
Tiger	:	Wild and crazy times together
Rabbit	:	If you can survive problem you make it
Dragon	:	Here a strong sexual bond
Snake	:	Even the passion is short termed
Horse	:	Short-term too much alike
Sheep	:	Made for each other, everlasting
Monkey	:	Friendship-yes, Marriage-no
Rooster	:	Lots of arguments but some hope
Dog	:	Lasting happiness and success
Pig	:	Only in the wildest dream could this be

METAL HORSE

Years of the Metal Horse: 1930, 1990, 2050

You have a fear of being trapped. And shun all forms of commitment. And you won't settle down until you find a stable relationship. You are a wild and untamed spirit.

Famous Metal Horses: Emma Watson, Anjli Mohindra, Samuel A. Alito Jr., David Archuleta, John Astin, Gene Hackman

WATER HORSE

Years of the Water Horse: 1942, 2002, 2062

Water horses can make the best out of any problem. And will adapt to make do. Changing their mind as the wind blows. Confusing both friends and business partner.

Famous Water Horses: Bob Hoskins, Al Jardine, Carole King, Graham Nash, Wayne Newton, Bobby Rydell, Martin Scorsese, David Ogden Stiers

WOOD HORSE

Years of the Wood Horse: 1954, 2014, 2074

Less skittish than most horses. Making them very predictable in a stable relationship. More likely to stick to the task at hand.

Famous Wood Horses: Michael Moore, Al Roker, Jim Beushi, Corbin Bernsen, Christie Brinkley

FIRE HORSE

Years of the Fire Horse: 1906, 1966, 2026

Wild streaks of the animal order. They are very unlucky in one group and the other very lucky. They not the ones to irritate if you can help it.

Famous Fire Horses: Bai Ling, Salma Hayek, Natalie Raitano, Justine Bateman, Dean Cain, Cindy Crawford

EARTH HORSE

Years of the Earth Horse: 1918, 1978, 2038

The stable minded and goal completer of the horses. But your fickle love. Life keeps you hoping from one to another.

Famous Earth Horses: Zoe Saldana, Nikki Cox, Beth Riestgraf, Nelly Furtado, Brian Urlacher, Ted Williams, Eddy Arnold, James Franco.

SHEEP

Easy going and known for going with the flow. They have an over need to care and nurture. Good providers and love of peace.

SHEEP FACTS

Eighth animal in the order

Chinese Name	:	Yang is the sign of arts
Month	:	July
Western Counterpart	:	Cancer
Color	:	Pink, Purple
Gemstones	:	Moonstone, Sapphire
Good Friends	:	Rabbits, Pigs
Bad Friends	:	Oxen

CHARACTERISTICS

Good : Artistry, Kindness, Gentleness, Sensitivity
Bad : Fussiness, Dependence, Self-indulgence

LOVE CONNECTION

Rat	:	At times this will be harder than it's worth
Ox	:	Never win this one, heart or mind
Tiger	:	Lots of respect but never marriage
Rabbit	:	Happiness through true love
Dragon	:	Could in up as hell or eden
Snake	:	Friends and lovers this is success
Horse	:	This mating will keep forever
Sheep	:	Placid meet placid, prefect lives
Monkey	:	Learning while you go will be your goal
Rooster	:	Hit and miss relationship
Dog	:	Personalities will cause problem
Pig	:	Love will make this love go round

METAL SHEEP

Years of the Metal Sheep: 1931, 1991, 2051

Sheep pretend to be hard, but their true feelings show them as soft and willing to be a friend. This heart of gold needs protecting of this outer shell. The love of art is strong here.

Famous Metal Sheep: Yasmin Page, Dan Rather, Mickey Mantle, Larry Hagman, Ian Holm

WATER SHEEP

Years of the Water Sheep: 1943, 2003, 2063

You're always content and able to get along with others. Always popular and well liked. They need to be safe and happy at home. They can be known to sulk, but they have a great sense of humor.

Famous Water Sheep: Joy Behar, Gary Burghoff, Blythe Danner

WOOD SHEEP

Years of the Wood Sheep: 1955, 2015, 2075

These busy sheep attract many friends and even more strays. You're always there to give comfort and compassion. You sometimes get over your head. It's good to put yourself first sometimes.

Famous Wood Sheep: Ken Safer, Chris Berman, Edwin Moses, Ellen Barkin, Dana Carvey, Rosanne Cash,

FIRE SHEEP

Years of the Fire Sheep: 1907, 1967, 2027

More outgoing and likes the support and approval of others. A strong natural sense of drama. You do well in the performing arts. And have a great social life and lots of friends.

Famous Fire Sheep: Lisa Bonet, Boris Becker, Criss Angel, Tia Carrere, Jeff Corwin, Nicole Kidman, Liz Phair, Julia Roberts, Mark Ruffalo

EARTH SHEEP

Years of the Earth Sheep: 1919, 1979, 2039

While a normally stable person, the sheep does lack in self-confidence. Naturally good in domesticated way. Working hard and always good to love ones.

Famous Earth Sheep: Norah Jones, Zhang Ziyi, Cote De Pablo, Maggie Q, Freeman Agyeman, Erica Cerra, Jennifer L. Hewitt, Rosario Dawson

MONKEY

The monkey is known for quick wits and mental dexterity. Keeping one step ahead of others in task. Good sense of fun and always looking for fresh challenges.

MONKEY FACTS

Ninth animal in the order

Chinese Name	:	HOU is the sign of imagination
Month	:	August
Western Counterpart	:	Leo
Color	:	Yellow, Gold
Gemstones	:	Aquamarine, Topaz, Agate
Good Friends	:	Dragons, Rats
Bad Friends	:	Tigers

CHARACTERISTICS

Good : Imagination, Sense of Humor, Versatility
Bad : Slyness, Restlessness, Mischievousness

LOVE CONNECTION

Rat	:	A good blend of love and understanding
Ox	:	When this is good it's fun
Tiger	:	You drive each other crazy
Rabbit	:	Heartbreak in the making
Dragon	:	Together in paradise
Snake	:	Emotions and jealousy may stop you
Horse	:	Bad sex in the future
Sheep	:	This match will success easily
Monkey	:	Forever teenager in actions
Rooster	:	In need of that romantic spark
Dog	:	If you desire you can make it work
Pig	:	Problems make the passions hotter

METAL MONKEY

Years of the Metal Monkey: 1920, 1980, 2040

Clever and persuasive, you are outwardly warm and strongly passionate in nature. Determined and strong willed, added to hard work will see you to success.

Famous Metal Monkeys: Zooey Deschanel, Christina Ricci, Eliza Dushka, Vanessa Ferlito, Christy Hemme, Kristen Bell

WATER MONKEY

Years of the Water Monkey: 1932, 1992, 2052

Keeping your feelings hidden. Rarely letting others know your plans. With patient methods they have success and will be natural trendsetters.

Famous Water Monkeys: Selena Gomez, Paulina Gaitman, Danielle A. Moberg, Jerry Vale, Elizabeth Taylor, Mel Tillis

WOOD MONKEY

Years of the Wood Monkey: 1944, 2004, 2064

Blessed with logic and a good understanding of the ways of life. You have a gift of communication and good well in the sciences.

Famous Wood Monkeys: James Carville Jr., Christopher Dodd, Steve Carlton, Tom Seaver, Jeff Beck, Richard Belzer, Gary Busey

FIRE MONKEY

Years of the Fire Monkey: 1956, 2016, 2076

With energy and stamina to match, you find a way to find a way to get the better of the situation.

Famous Fire Monkeys: Robby Benson, David Caruso, Gary Cole, Sinbad, Sela Ward, Montel Williams

EARTH MONKEY

Years of the Earth Monkey: 1908, 1968, 2028

Honest, very serious, and known for their intelligence. More dependable than other monkeys. You appreciate respect and hate when it's not given. You are a kind and loyal lover.

Famous Earth Monkeys: Halle Berry, Kristin Chenoweth, Stacey Dash, Kylie Minogue, Kelly Hu, Lucy Liu

ROOSTER

Strong-willed and confident, the Roosters are show-off and likes to strut their stuff. Unlike Snakes, Roosters are not given to underhanded or trickery in their dealing. Very blunt and straightforward.

ROOSTER FACTS

Tenth animal in the order

Chinese Name	:	JI is the sign of honesty
Month	:	September
Western Counterpart	:	Virgo
Color	:	Peach, Apricot
Gemstones	:	Diamond, Ruby, Topaz
Best Friends	:	Oxen, Snakes
Bad Friends	:	Rabbits

CHARACTERISTICS

Good : Resilience, Courage, Passion, Patriotism
Bad : Bluntness, Conceit, Rudeness, Bossiness

LOVE CONNECTION

Rat	:	Lots of problems but a tender love
Ox	:	Sex, love and happiness
Tiger	:	Get talking for success
Rabbit	:	Opposites do not work
Rooster	:	A bomb waiting to go off
Dragon	:	Fun but lots of ego problems
Snake	:	Shows sides of true love
Horse	:	Power conflicts but a good pair
Sheep	:	Good union, lots of success
Monkey	:	No romance lives here
Dog	:	Difficult in the making
Pig	:	Fight hard and this could work

METAL ROOSTER

Years of the Metal Rooster: 1921, 1981, 2041

Cocky with a large ego but with great skills of deduction and the ability to analyze most things. And will work to improve the humankind any way he can.

Famous Metal Roosters: Rinko Kikuchi, Beyonce, Jessica Alba, Alexis Beldel, Hannah Spearritt, Natalie Portman, Alicia Keys, Summer Glau, Tila Tequila

WATER ROOSTER

Years of the Water Rooster: 1933, 1993, 2053

Quieter, calmer and usually more intellectual than normal roosters. You are a constant supply of energy. But will get sidetracked on tasks.

Famous Water Roosters: Alyson Stoner, Gene Wilder, Wayne Rogers, Joan Rivers, Roman Polanski, Willie Nelson, Kim Novak

WOOD ROOSTER

Years of the Wood Rooster: 1945, 2005, 2065

Kind and considerate, always well-liked by family and friends. Having a strong conscience and will work hard for good causes. Forgetting not everyone and has the energy to keep up with them. Being too critical to some people.

Famous Wood Roosters: Rod Carew, Dirk Benedict, David Brenner, Eric Clapton, Rita Coolidge, Tony Dow, Mia Farrow

FIRE ROOSTER

Years of the Fire Rooster: 1957, 2017, 2077

You are prone to display of theatricals and spend a lot of time caring about your looks. Your willpower makes you a leader and great organizer. Keep an eye, you don't bully others.

Famous Fire Roosters: Daniel Day-Lewis, Maria Conchita Alonso, Stephen Fry, Leeza Gibbons, Vince Gill, John Turturro, Mario Van Peebles

EARTH ROOSTER

Years of the Earth Rooster: 1909, 1969, 2029

Careful, neat and efficient. You also have a good sense of goal or takes on the responsibility.

Famous Earth Roosters: Gwen Stefani, Pauley Perrette, Barry Bradley, Maggie Chueg, Christian Slater, Christy Turlington, Julianna Marguiles

DOG

You are one of the great caretakers of the universe. Willing to make time for others. You are unselfish and very caring.

DOG FACTS

Eleventh animal in the order

Chinese Name	:	GOU is the sign of fidelity
Month	:	October
Western Counterpart	:	Libra
Color	:	Pale Yellow
Gemstones	:	Moonstone, Carnelian, Jasper
Good Friends	:	Tigers, Horses
Bad Friends	:	Dragons

CHARACTERISTICS

Good : Reliability, Honesty, Devotion, Unselfishness
Bad : Anxiety, Cynicism, Nosiness, Pessimism

LOVE CONNECTION

Rat	:	Boring but solid
Ox	:	Small to no chance of happiness
Tiger	:	A good relationship for two
Rabbit	:	Good and solid
Dragon	:	Retreat is not surrender
Snake	:	Love at first sight
Horse	:	This one can last forever
Sheep	:	Egos will clash
Monkey	:	Your desire will keep this one going
Rooster	:	Difficulties will arise
Dog	:	Deepest affection, understanding
Pig	:	Honest and sincere in partnerships

METAL DOG

Years of the Metal Dog: 1910, 1970, 2030

High standards, loyal and faithful. Needs help looking to lighten up.

Famous Metal Dogs: Rachel Wiesz, Charmisa Carpenter, Amy O'Donnell, Queen Latifah, Leah Remini

WATER DOG

Years of the Water Dog: 1922, 1982, 2042

Flexible and easy going. More in need of control than other dogs. But never have a small list of friends.

Famous Water Dogs: Kimberly Wyatt, Devok Aoki, Lacey Chabert, Jessica Biel, Anne Hathaway, Reiko Suho, Kimberly Caldwell, Abbie Connish

WOOD DOG

Years of the Wood Dog: 1934, 1994, 2054

Generous nature and well balanced. More likely to work with groups, disliking being alone.

Famous Wood Dogs: Mark Indelicato, Alan Arkin, Brigitte Bardot, Justin Bieber, Pat Boone, Richard Chamberlain

FIRE DOG

Years of the Fire Dog: 1946, 2006, 2066

Born leaders with a strong streak of adventure. With tons of charm and charismatic. Known to get carried away with success. This one dog has a more volatile nature than others.

Famous Fire Dogs: Darnell Trotter, John Woo, Demond Wilson, Ben Vereen, John Waters, Joe Spano, Steven Spielberg, Linda Ronstadt

EARTH DOG

Years of the Earth Dog: 1958, 2018, 2078

Slow but sure, you are wise and kind. Good at giving advice in money matters. A good influence on others with their quiet persuasive nature.

Famous Earth Dogs: Jack Abramoff, Christine Brennan, Mark Cuban, Kevin Bacon. Bruce Campbell, Steve Guttenberg, Patricia Heaton

BOAR

Naturally patient and cheerful. You feel the need to brighten up others around you. At times you can be too trusting but you seldom hold a grudge. Happy to share with others. A real down to earth and happy spirit.

BOAR FACTS

Twelfth animal in the order

Chinese Name	:	ZHU is the sign of honesty
Month	:	November
Western Counterpart	:	Scorpio
Color	:	Dark Blue
Gemstones	:	Lapis lazuli, Coral, Beryl
Best Friends	:	Rabbits, Sheep
Bad Friends	:	Snake

CHARACTERISTICS

Good : Sincerity, Diligence, Generosity
Bad : Naivety, Materialism, Laziness, Pigheadedness

LOVE CONNECTION

Rat	:	Lots of ups and downs, better friends
Ox	:	Worth the risk
Tiger	:	Good humor keeps this union moving
Rabbit	:	A shared happiness and bliss
Dragon	:	Deeply loving relationship
Snake	:	This is a deep and wide division
Horse	:	Way too laid back to work well
Sheep	:	Love and understanding make happiness go well
Monkey	:	This affair will be loud and passionate
Rooster	:	Work at this it's worth it
Dog	:	Solid but dull relationship
Boar	:	Chances are 50/50

METAL BOAR

Years of the Metal Boar: 1911, 1971, 2031

Passionate and loving, he puts 100 percent into all he does. Not endowed with good judgment when it's about others.

Famous Metal Boars: Winona Ryder, Leila Rourass, Shannen Dorherty, Patricia Velasquez, Lance Armstrong, Janet Evans, Picabo Street, Kurt Warner

WATER BOAR

Years of the Water Boar: 1923, 1983, 2043

While more adept at dealing with people than other boars you're still too trusting. Helpful and kind you like to be of service. A keen mind serves you well in business.

Famous Water Boars: Jamie Chung, Samantha Mumba, Alexa Chueg, Mila Kunis, Adrienne Palicki, Aikawa Yuzuki

WOOD BOAR

Years of the Wood Boar: 1935, 1995, 2055

When handling people, you have a gift of diplomacy that could make a saint proud. You give money and time to good charitable causes and are willing to apply yourself harder than most to get success.

Famous Wood Boars: Mickey Wright, Gary Player, Frank Robinson, Woody Allen, Julie Andrews, Diahann Carroll, Robert Conrad, Phil Donahue

FIRE BOAR

Years of the Fire Boar: 1947, 2007, 2067

Capable of doing and understanding acts of heroism. Once set, nothing will stop him from his course. This boar is given to impulsively and bold risks.

Famous Fire Boars: Gregg Allman, Anne Archer, Meredith Baxter, David Bowie, Albert Brooks, Billy Crystal, Stephen Collins, Michael Gross

EARTH BOAR

Years of the Earth Boar: 1959, 2019, 2079

Easy-going and sensible, bound to be happy with family and friends. Believes in keeping organized. With low ambition, you are happy with the simple ways of life. But watch; you don't overindulge.

Famous Earth Boars: Bradley Whitford, Colin Quinn, Martha Quinn, Ving Rhames, Adrain Paul, Mackenzie Phillips, Bronson Pinchot, Judd Nelson, Marie Osmond

www.ingramcontent.com/pod-product-compliance
Lightning Source LLC
Chambersburg PA
CBHW051248110526
44588CB00025B/2917